Mum Skunk and Scamp the Dog

By Sally Cowan

Two skunk kits are snug in the nest.

"It is damp out there, my kits!" said Mum.

Mum left the kits to rest.
Then she went out
in the mist to hunt.

Mum was glad to see some plump black slugs on a clump of plants.

She jumps and plucks them off!

Mum yanks grubs from the soft land.

Then Mum drank from a dish.

But Scamp the dog snuck up on Mum!

Scamp had not met a skunk.

He bent to sniff Mum.

Mum is cross!

Mum grunts and stomps!

Flick, flick!

Mum shot mist at Scamp!

Mum ran back to her kits.

Scamp fled to the fish pond to get the mist off!

CHECKING FOR MEANING

1. What did Mum find on her hunt? *(Literal)*
2. Where did Scamp go to wash off the stinky mist? *(Literal)*
3. Why did Mum shoot mist at Scamp? *(Inferential)*

EXTENDING VOCABULARY

rest	What sounds are in the word *rest*? Which other word in the story rhymes with *rest*? Which sounds in these two words are the same? Which are different?
yanks	In the story, Mum yanks grubs from the land. What is another word for *yank*?
cross	What does the word *cross* mean in the story? What is another word the author could have used?

MOVING BEYOND THE TEXT

1. A baby skunk is called a kit. What other animals call their babies kits?
2. Skunks use a stinky spray, or mist, to protect themselves. Why would a stinky spray scare away predators?
3. What would you do if you saw a skunk?
4. What are some ways that other animals protect themselves from danger?

SPEED SOUNDS

PRACTICE WORDS